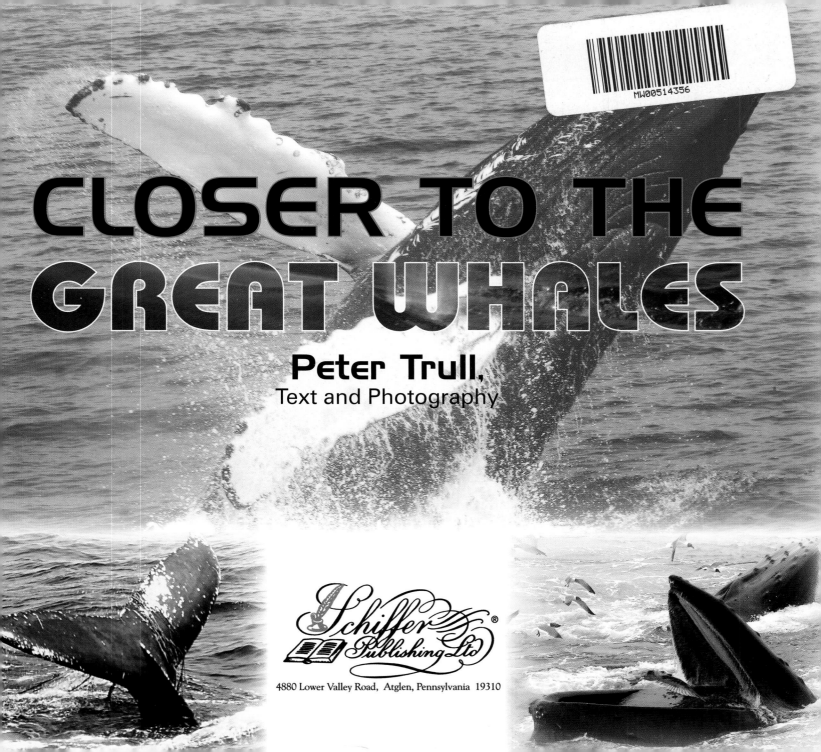

CLOSER TO THE
GREAT WHALES

Peter Trull,
Text and Photography

Schiffer Publishing Ltd

4880 Lower Valley Road, Atglen, Pennsylvania 19310

Dedication

This book is dedicated to all those who are mystified by, and dream about, the sight of the eye from above.

Designed by Mark David Bowyer
Type set in HandelGothic BT / Zurich BT

ISBN: 978-0-7643-3507-5
Printed in China

Schiffer Books are available at special discounts for bulk purchases for sales promotions or premiums. Special editions, including personalized covers, corporate imprints, and excerpts can be created in large quantities for special needs. For more information contact the publisher:

Published by Schiffer Publishing Ltd.
4880 Lower Valley Road
Atglen, PA 19310
Phone: (610) 593-1777; Fax: (610) 593-2002
E-mail: Info@schifferbooks.com

For the largest selection of fine reference books on this and related subjects, please visit our web site at **www.schifferbooks.com**
We are always looking for people to write books on new and related subjects. If you have an idea for a book please contact us at the above address.

This book may be purchased from the publisher.
Include $5.00 for shipping.
Please try your bookstore first.
You may write for a free catalog.

In Europe, Schiffer books are distributed by
Bushwood Books
6 Marksbury Ave.
Kew Gardens
Surrey TW9 4JF England
Phone: 44 (0) 20 8392 8585; Fax: 44 (0) 20 8392 9876
E-mail: info@bushwoodbooks.co.uk
Website: www.bushwoodbooks.co.uk

Contents

Acknowledgments

An enthusiastic thank you goes out to all of the people who helped me complete this project. Thanks to Pete Schiffer at Schiffer Publishing Ltd. for his willingness to listen and his patience. Thanks also to Jeff Snyder and Douglas Congdon-Martin, also of Schiffer Publishing, for their help and guidance through the process of completing this book. Thanks to all who helped me learn about and appreciate the great whales, Al Avellar, Aaron Avellar, Dr. Phil Clapham, Dr. Stormy Mayo, Dave Matilla, Ed Lyman, Margaret Murphy, Marilyn Marx, and Tim Cole. A ton of gratitude goes to Dr. Jooke Robbins and Scott Landry who helped me with photographic interpretation, and a sincere thank you to Dr. Carole Carlson for providing patience, understanding, and several other factors which have kept me going in a fairly straight line. Immeasurable thanks go to Steve Milliken, captain and owner of Dolphin Fleet Whale Watch. There is no way this project could have been completed without the love, patience, and guidance of my incredible wife Carol. It was also Carol Trull and Blair Nikula who gave so much of their time with technical help in photography. Thanks also to the folks at Orleans Camera and Video.

I must sing praise to all of the captains of whale watch vessels that I have worked with over the years. They are the highly skilled, caring professionals, who allow millions of people to have life changing experiences on the open seas. Operating vessels around these enormous, endangered, seemingly unconcerned cetaceans with such skill shows compassion and toughness. And I'm proud to be associated with all of the naturalists who teach people on board about the whales and marine environment while photographing and recording data. A tip of the hat goes to all of those interns and volunteers who give their time and who volunteer as data collectors on board, especially Alexa Hilmer and Jamie Fitzgerald.

The author expresses extreme gratitude to the Provincetown Center for Coastal Studies, Provincetown, Massachusetts, for permission to use photographic images in this book.

The author is also extremely grateful to the Dolphin Fleet Whale Watch, Provincetown, Massachusetts, for permission to use photographic images in this book.

Foreword

Few people have ever seen one of the "Great Whales." With one exception, they are the whales of the world that have the feeding apparatus called baleen in their mouths. These whales are generally represented by the rorquals and the right whales, as well as the Pacific Ocean gray whale. True to their name, they are some of the largest animals that have ever lived on earth. The one *Odontoceti*, or toothed whale, that fits into this category is the great square-headed sperm whale.

Most people around the world, who have had the opportunity to observe these whales have done so on commercial whale watches, cruise ships, or fishing vessels. While there are areas where they can be seen from shore, vessels that carry people into the open ocean to their feeding or breeding grounds offer the best opportunity for viewing these magnificent animals, sometimes at very close range. These spottings are often of limited time and people may not be sure what part of the enormous mass they are actually seeing. When the whale surfaces to breathe, then slips below the surface, we don't see the whole animal at one time; rather we see various parts—a blow hole, some dark, smooth skin, a fin, maybe a tail. Where's the whale? It's too big to see!

In these pages, aspects of the whales that are not typically seen or described in detail to most observers are shown in detail. The awesome, sometimes emotional observations in the open sea are too fleeting to interpret in what is often just a few, quick observations! Many times, no, most times, the details of the animal are missed. Here, through words and photographic images, the reader will see and learn about aspects of whales' natural history, ranging from anatomical features and feeding adaptations, to sensory perception and factors limiting survival. All of the photographs were made by the author off the coast of New England and more specifically in the waters around Cape Cod. This book will introduce you to the great world and bring you closer to the great whales.

Welcome to the World of Whales

A Hole In The Ocean. A fifty-ton humpback whale hits the sea surface after a full spinning head breach. The whale jumped from the water, spun in the air, and landed on its back, hitting the water with tremendous force. The image shows the throat pleats of the whale, looking forward to barnacles on the chin (bottom). Its huge mass has created a seven-foot deep hole and a wall below the surface. The white downward streaks in the water wall are from rough spots on the whale's chin, likely clusters of barnacles.

The earth's oceans cover just over seventy percent of the planet's surface and there are many great mysteries that lie beneath the waves. Some of the most enigmatic of these are the whales, free roaming, oxygen-breathing mammals that have evolved to a life under the waters surface. Found in all oceans of the world, cetaceans, which include whales, dolphins, and porpoises, evolved from land-dwelling mammals that probably looked something like our present day hippopotamus, and took to the water about 40-45 million years ago.

The word *Cetacea* is derived from the Greek word *ketos*, meaning large sea animal, and *cetus*, Latin for a whale or large sea creature. In terms of animal classification, *Cetacea* refers to the order, in the class *Mammalia*. These graceful, intelligent marine creatures are divided into two distinct groups, or suborders, the *Odontoceti* and the *Mysticeti*. Like the term *Cetacea*, these descriptive terms are also derived from Greek and Latin, and each refers to the type of feeding apparatus inside the whale's mouth. The *Odontoceti* are the toothed whales, primarily dolphins and porpoises, the largest of which is the sperm whale, *Physeter macrocephalus*, the great square headed *Cetacean* made familiar to us by the classic story *Moby Dick*, by Herman Melville. Perhaps more familiar to us is the killer whale, *Orcinus orca*, a species kept in captivity around the world and often used to demonstrate the intelligence of marine mammals through exhibitions and shows. When I watch these shows, I often wonder who is training whom. Are the whales training the humans to feed them?

Aside from these two familiar species of toothed whales, the *Odontocetes* are best represented by the large diversity of dolphins and porpoises found in the world's oceans. These range from the small harbor porpoise, about four feet long, to the aforementioned sperm whale, which ranges up to 50 feet in length. Like all of the *Cetacea*, the *Odontoceti* are smooth-skinned, hydrodynamic mammals that range the oceans of the world,

feeding mainly on fish, squid, and small euphausiid shrimp called krill. Killer whales deviate from that general description, killing and eating other whale species as well as a variety of pinnipeds, seals and sea lions.

Dolphins and porpoises differ in three principal features related to body shape and form; the rostrum, dorsal fin, and the shape of the teeth. Dolphins tend to have a more pronounced rostrum, or beak, while the front of a porpoise head most often appears blunt or rounded. A second difference is the shape of the dorsal fin, the fin in the middle of the back, which helps to stabilize the animal as it swims. On a dolphin, the dorsal fin has a falcate shape, rather like a shark's fin, pointed and backward pointing, while porpoises tend to have more triangular shaped dorsal fins. The third principal difference between dolphins and porpoises is the shape of the teeth. Like all *Odontoceti*, the teeth and jaws in both are designed to grasp and hold their prey. Since no chewing takes places as they feed, all *Odontocete* teeth are similar in shape with variations. A dolphin displays cone-like, or conical, teeth, pointed and sharp in both the upper and lower jaw. While the orientation of teeth in a porpoise is similar, the shape of their teeth is flat and spade-like. Other differences between the two *Odontoceti* include body shape, social structure, and pod size, but these three anatomical structures are most descriptive in defining the differences between dolphins and porpoises.

The second of the suborders is the *Mysticeti*, which are the subjects of this book. The term *Mysticeti* refers to the moustache-like appearance of the baleen plates that extend from the upper jaw of these whales. The descriptive term of this suborder is likely derived from the Greek word *mystakos*, for mustache. The reader need only observe the photographs in the section on baleen to grasp that concept. The diversity of *Mysticeti* in the world's oceans is considerably less than that of the *Odontoceti* (11 species of baleen whales compared to about 67 species of toothed whales). Although the baleen whales are divided into four distinct groups, or families, only two, the rorquals *(Balaenopteridae)* and the right whales *(Balaenidae)* are represented here. The gray whale *(Eschrichtiidae)* is only found in the Pacific Ocean and has not been photographed by the author (a Cape Codder), and the pygmy right whale *(Neobalaenidae)* of the southern hemisphere is a species about which very little is known.

Rorqual is a Norwegian term referring to the throat grooves found in the humpback whale, blue whale, minke whale, finback whale, sei whale, and Bryde's whale. Bryde's whale *(Balaenoptera edeni)*, found in tropical and semi-tropical waters, is not represented here.

The Great Food Filter – Baleen

Remember that the *Mysticeti* differ from the *Odontoceti* in that, rather than grasping one or a few food items at a time with their teeth and then swallowing, humpback, finback, and other rorqual whales lunge or swim through huge schools of fish or patches of plankton, taking tremendous volumes of food and water into their mouths. When they feed this way, pleats of skin on the lower jaw and throat that extend from the chin to the navel (yes, whales are mammals and have belly-buttons) distend outward like a great pelican's pouch. An animal that is most often thought of as a long, streamlined, and hydrodynamic, takes on the appearance of a big, balloon-headed creature whose dump truck-sized mouth and throat are filled with thousands of gallons of water and hundreds of pounds of small fish. They must then separate the water and food by getting all of that water out of their mouths without losing the precious food that they have expended tremendous amounts of energy to catch.

A Closer Look at Baleen. The next four images provide detailed views of baleen and the role it plays in the feeding strategies and behavior of whales.

This image, taken directly at the rostrum or front of a humpback whale jaw with its mouth partially open, shows how this group got their name. An ancient mariner looking into the mouth of this great leviathan could easily see the "mustache." These are the shortest of the baleen plates which become longer toward the gape of the mouth.

This view from the side of an open-mouthed humpback whale shows the singular, side-by-side arrangement of baleen plates as they hang from the upper jaw. Each single, vertical dark line represents a flat plate of baleen. Water can be seen flowing through the plates, trapping small fish, although a few can be seen wriggling out of the whale's huge, bucket-like lower jaw. The far rim of the lower jaw is visible just to the left of the shortest baleen plates at the front of the mouth.

A view into the open mouth of a feeding humpback whale. The pink roof of the mouth, or pallet, is visible as the main feature, while water streams off the fibrous backside of the baleen. The bulging lower jaw, still filled with water, is being closely scanned by an immature herring gull. The frothing, emerald green water is the result of a massive bubble cloud created by the whale as a means to force small fish to the surface.

Opposite page:
Here again we see the front, short baleen plates in a slightly opened mouth. Other features on the jaw line tell a story about this individual whale. Hair follicles, barnacle scars and "left handed" scuffing abrasions are all visible in this straight on image. Notice the water pouring from the distended lower jaw at the gape of the mouth. Water is sifted through the baleen plates, and while we see that the lower jaw is full of water, none flows out without being filtered by the baleen. This forward movement and draining of water is called "dragging." Dragging also uses the pressure of the sea water against the chin to flatten out the flexible, distended throat grooves. *Photo courtesy of Dolphin Fleet Whale, Provincetown, Massachusetts.*

Hanging from the upper jaw, inside the mouths of the whale, is a curtain of hundreds of baleen plates. The baleen plates, hanging side-by-side from the upper jaw, in the same horseshoe-shaped orientation as teeth in other mammals, have hairy fibers on the back side which trap the food, preventing it from going between the plates of baleen as the water is pushed out of the whale's mouth with the tongue. The water flows between the hundreds of plates of baleen out of the mouth while the food is trapped behind it, and then swallowed. These plates create a sieve, a filter separating a myriad of food items from the water.

To get a better idea of this feeding process, imagine that you have a bulging mouthful of rice and water. Now you want to get the water out of your mouth without swallowing it or loosing any of the rice. So you clench your teeth and use your tongue to push the water out of your mouth. It escapes between your clenched teeth, trapping the rice kernels behind them until all the water is gone and you swallow the rice.

In whales, the food items that are captured in the baleen range from microscopic zooplankton like copepods, fish, and other animal larvae and small shrimp-like crustaceans, called krill, to fish several inches long. Humpback whales and finback whales will eat fish as large as mackerel and herring.

Baleen or "whalebone," as it was called historically, is not bone at all. The long flexible plates are made from a protein called keratin, the same material as fingernails, hair, horse's hoofs and cow's horns. The length of the plates hanging from the upper jaws of the great whales range in size from several inches in the small minke whale, looking like a small whisk, to the ten to eleven feet long thin plates hanging from the upper jaw of the critically endangered North Atlantic right whale. During the Victorian Era, the mid- to late 1800s, whale baleen was used for a large variety of everyday items ranging from ladies' corsets to horse brushes, combs, buggy whips, furniture inlay, and umbrella spokes.

Behaviors

A curtain of white hangs on the horizon. Miles away we see the poof of whale spouts in the windless air, too far away to formulate an animals shape, but clear evidence of what lies below these great billowing breaths.

"Thar' she blows!" was the call of whalers. For centuries the sight of spouts on the horizon led profiteering men onward, slaughtering mind-boggling numbers of cetaceans for oil and baleen. Today, the sight of spouts on the horizon brings shouts of excitement and tears of joy as people anticipate the moment in their lives when they see one of the largest and rarest animals on earth.

In the waters off Cape Cod it is most often the humpback whale, whose exhalations dot the horizon like cotton balls on any summer day. Carbon dioxide gas exhaled from the lungs, mucous, condensed water vapor and standing water blasted from the concave "bowl" created by the closed nostrils and surrounding splashguard, all blend to create the blow or spout, shooting upwards at over *200 mph*!

It is this spout, this upward blasting plume, that whale watching vessels in over one-hundred countries around the world search for as they venture forth to educate and inspire people with lasting impressions with hopes of getting closer to the great whales. The next seven images are of various views and aspects of the whale spouts.

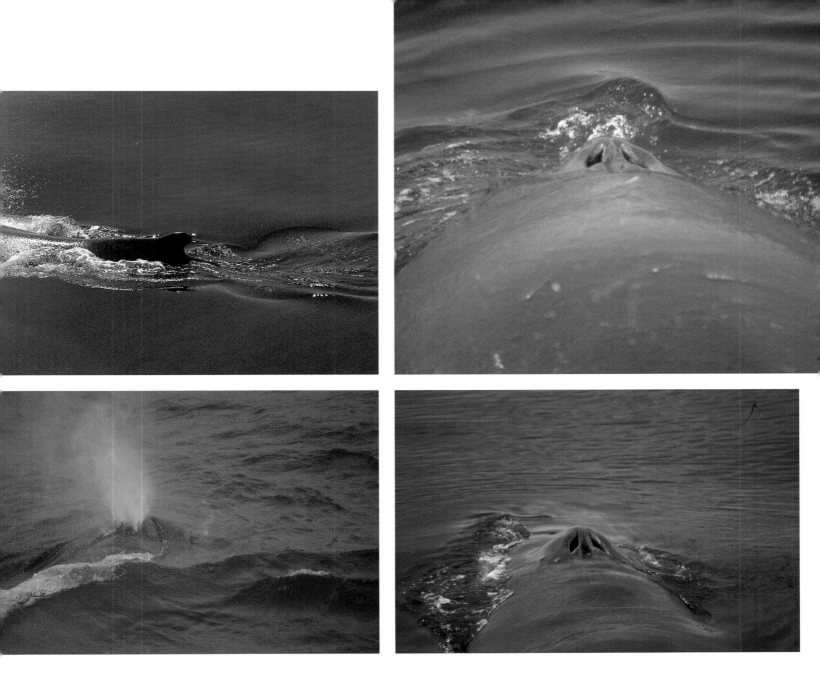

Whales, especially humpback whales, carry out a variety of recognizable and named surface behaviors that are among the most exciting and spectacular sights in the animal kingdom. The most well known, often seen in film, video, and photographs, is the spinning head breach. Here, a whale rises from below the oceans surface in a jump that may take 75 percent or more of its body mass out of the water, spins with white pectoral flippers flailing, then crashes down on its side or back, creating one of the biggest splashes any animal could ever make. Despite the many times it has been shown on television, seeing it in a natural setting on the open sea is considered a rare sight.

In the following six images we see examples of three of the most common surface behaviors: breaching, lob-tailing and flipper-slapping. The reasons for these behaviors remain unknown, although researchers have suggested a number of motives for this and other spectacular surface behaviors that occur at any seemingly random times. Some possible reasons for these extraordinary displays include:

- Knocking off any form of ectoparasites like cyamids, small crustaceans that may irritate the skin
- Knocking of barnacles, which, though not parasitic, may irritate the skin
- Communicating with other cetaceans through loud surface smashes
- Breathing more easily in rough seas
- Stimulating the movement of food through the digestive system
- Dislodging small food fish from between the baleen plates
- Exerting dominance over other whales
- Immobilizing small prey
- Knocking off dead skin from the body
- Play—sheer jubilance

A spinning head breach occurs more frequently on days when the wind is blowing and the seas are rough. Some breaches are high and strong, with the whale shooting straight up into the air. Others are lazy, the whale lunging more sideways out of the water. In either case, the sight of a whale breaching is a once-in-a-lifetime observation for many people. *Photos courtesy of Dolphin Fleet Whale, Provincetown, Massachusetts.*

Lob tailing or tail lobbing is a behavior that occurs when a whale, here a humpback, either lies on the surface, oblique to the surface or straight up and down, with its head under water raising and slapping its flukes on the surface, creating a big splash and a loud crash or thump. Interestingly, the whale may lob tail when lying on its back, as if doing an abdominal crunch, and crashing the dorsal surface of the fluke on the water, or while lying normally at the surface and stretching the vertebrae in a U and crashing the ventral surface.

Although these humpbacks appear very vertical in position, they are using the ventral surface of the fluke to make the crash. *Photos courtesy of Dolphin Fleet Whale, Provincetown, Massachusetts.*

A humpback slamming its dorsal fluke on the surface. *Photo courtesy of Dolphin Fleet Whale, Provincetown, Massachusetts.*

Flipper slapping occurs when a whale turns on its side, raises its pectoral flipper above the surface, then slams it down on the water creating a loud crash. I think the sound of flipper slapping carries farther, at least above the surface, than any other surface behavior. When a humpback flipper slaps, we see another distinctive pattern of black and white pigmentation that is distinctive on every whale. It is difficult to use for identification, however, as the flipper is usually under water, but these patterns are beautiful and unique. It is during this behavior that it is easiest to see the eye of these great cetaceans. When observing a whale flipper slapping, look immediately in front of where the flipper joins the body.

Photo courtesy of Dolphin Fleet Whale, Provincetown, Massachusetts.

Laughing gulls and black-legged kittiwakes are reflected in the shiny wet back of a feeding humpback whale. While the whale is working to find and corral food in a series of bubble clouds, the birds glide and hover just overhead, creating an artistic mosaic of reflection.

Herring gulls ride on the rostrum of a humpback whale. After feeding, as the whale prepares to dive again, gulls conserve energy by riding on the only object above the water, in close proximity to the next whale-provided banquet. Note the bloody, scratched, and scarred upper jaw of the whale. These superficial wounds occur when the whale scuffs the bottom with its upper jaw, swimming at an angle oblique to the bottom, with its tail up and head down, in a type of feeding strategy to exploit sand eels, which often burrow into bottom sediment. White pigment on a whale's dark skin in the wound areas is scarring.

Before lunging to the surface with an open mouth, a humpback whale must locate small fish using visual and auditory cues. Small pencil-shaped silvery fish called a sand lances (*Ammodytae* spp.) swim in dense schools, numbering tens of thousands, that are exploited not only by whales, but by a great diversity of predatory fish like cod, haddock, flounder, striped bass, bluefish, and tuna. In order to catch a large amount of small fish with as little effort as possible, humpback whales corral the sand lances into dense, tight schools by surrounding them with columns of bubbles. Swimming below the fish, blowing a circle of bubble columns around the school, and lunging through the tight school with mouth wide open is a feeding strategy that benefits the great whales.

Here we see a detailed close-up of the wounds and abrasions caused by bottom scuffing. The bottom sediment on Stellwagen Bank is sandy and, in some areas, covered with shards of shells and shell debris. Humpback whales use their upper and lower jaws to scrape or scuff the bottom, driving the sand eels out of the sediment and making them easier for the whales to exploit. Clearly, this causes some abrasions to the skin on the jaws of the whale and, as can be seen here, hair follicles are rubbed flat on the lower jaw. It is not uncommon to see a foot or more of red, raw abrasions on a humpback whale's upper jaw on top of white scar tissue that is likely from years of this type of feeding. In this image, note the three large abrasions and the white scar tissue scuffed and torn. Water pours out of the whale's mouth as a herring gull takes off with a sand eel. *Photo courtesy of Dolphin Fleet Whale, Provincetown, Massachusetts.*

Using pigmentation patterns on the ventral flukes of humpback whales to recognize individuals would be only one of several methods of identification if whales showed more of their body during their daily routines. But no other body part is as predictably evident as the fluke, which is raised when the whale dives after a breathing sequence at the surface. Many humpbacks also can be recognized by their dorsal fins as they glide along at the surface. Here, like white painted bubbles, barnacle scars on the chin of this humpback might aid in identifying this individual, but these scars may fade over the years. Barnacle scars, the baleen "mustache," hair follicles and a small scuffing scar are all visible on this individual.

Here, on the dorsal fin of a juvenile humpback whale, barnacles get a free ride around the North Atlantic Ocean. Barnacles drift through the water in their planktonic stage, until a platform for attachment, such as a whale body, presents itself, carrying the barnacle to nutrient rich feeding areas. Whales are constantly seeking food, often in the form of plankton eating fish, thereby providing these hitchhiking crustaceans with nutrients. This may be seen as another form of commensalism, where two organisms benefit from the behavior of one without negative outcomes to either animal. Note the white pigment, likely some form of scarring, over the dorsal fin. *Photo courtesy of Dolphin Fleet Whale, Provincetown, Massachusetts.*

Whales inhale and exhale the same atmospheric oxygen that we do, the difference being that we breathe unconsciously, without thinking about it or even being aware of the constant turnover of gasses in our lungs. This is not the case with the great whales. They live under water. Without gills, they must raise their nostrils, called blow holes, above the fluidic plain and inhale. Their lungs expand to a much higher capacity than humans and they respire with greater efficiency and use of the oxygen. When their lungs are filled, they consciously seal their blowholes, holding their breath until they surface again. Then they open their blowholes above the surface and blast carbon dioxide from their lungs in a loud and powerful gas exchange called a spout. This spout is made up of water and carbon dioxide and condensed water vapor from the lungs rising in a tall, white, cloud.

Because whales have to be conscious of their breathing, they don't sleep; they can't. Instead they rest at the surface, breathing slowly, in an appropriately named behavior called "logging." Here, four humpbacks log peacefully and still in a calm summer sea.

A baleen whale's nostrils have no connection to the esophagus, so the whale cannot breathe through its mouth. When humans breathe, air flows from the nostrils or mouths to the lungs via the pharynx and trachea. When we eat, because the esophagus is posterior to the trachea, a small flap called the epiglottis blocks the opening to the trachea so that our food doesn't get sucked into our lungs.

When a large whale like a humpback takes a breath, a series of events occur in order. The whale rises and breaks the surface with its blowholes. A large muscular splashguard rises to prevent water from flowing into the nostrils as the whale exhales carbon dioxide and water vapor. The water vapor condenses into droplets upon contact with cool air at the ocean surface. This condensed water vapor, as well as water resting in the blowhole cavity area is blasted skyward, creating a white plume called a spout or blow, which is often visible for miles. Immediately after the exhalation or blow, the blowholes open even wider as the whale draws a tremendous volume of oxygen into its lungs. A good listener can often hear that inhalation, like a great vacuum. All of this takes place over a few seconds as the whale surfaces and breathes in a series of 4-6 breaths.

In forward motion all the while, after inhalation, the blowholes close, the splashguard flattens, and water flows over the whale's dorsal surface as it submerges. While on a dive, its lungs filled with oxygen, a whale's heart rate slows, its blood concentrates in areas where oxygen use is highest, the brain, heart and lungs, and a protein chemical called myglobin in the muscle tissue stores oxygen, allowing for the cetacean to stay submerged for several minutes.

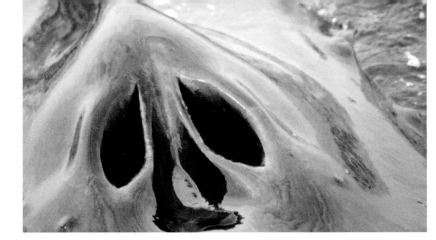

A look straight down into the blowholes.

A forward look down the dorsal surface to the raised splashguard and blowholes

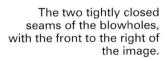

The two tightly closed seams of the blowholes, with the front to the right of the image.

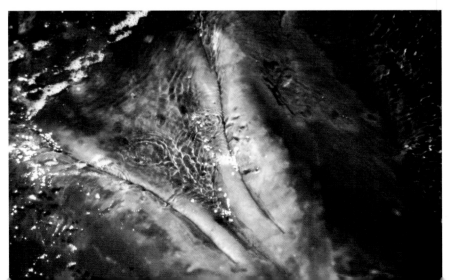

27

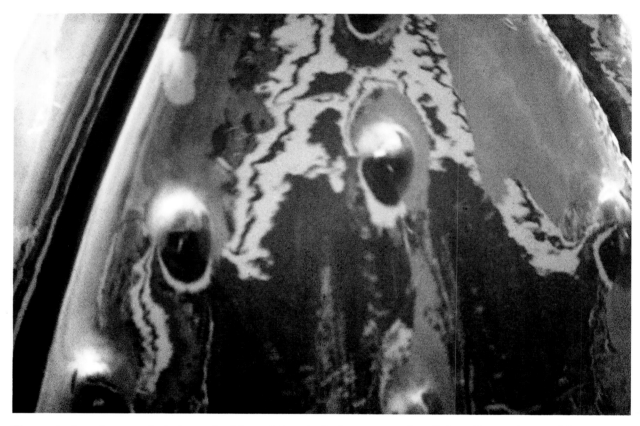

The ancient mariners and whalers called them "stove bolts," some people call them "goose bumps," but the correct term is tubercle. They are the hair follicles found most noticeably on the chin and head of humpback whales. Whales are mammals and, like all mammals, they have hair. The full covering of hair on the body is gone, lost as part of their evolution from land animals to a hydrodynamic sea-dwelling mammals. However, the remnants of hair, perhaps acting as sensory features on the body of these great whales, are evident as golf ball-sized bumps, some with a single hair protruding.

Here, a few of these bristly hairs are clearly evident as a humpback whale "spy hops," lifting its head straight out of the water, in this case, right in front of my telephoto lens. The colors reflected in the wet skin of the top of this whale's head are from the brightly colored clothes of people on a whale watch boat. Following strict guidelines, whale watch captains let their vessels drifting out of gear when they are near whales. They may suddenly have their passengers rewarded with a once-in-a-lifetime observation as a humpback whale, perhaps curious, surfaces directly beside the vessel. Always have the camera ready!

Sand eels.

Feeding on small fish is the daily objective of both the humpback whale and the laughing gull. Finding a feeding situation where the least degree of energy is expended for a relatively high degree of food is the optimum situation. In the following seven images, the whales drive small fish to the surface and the gulls and shearwaters glide effortlessly overhead, occasionally picking fish from the surface.

Herring gulls, laughing gulls, black-legged kittiwakes, greater shearwaters, and sooty shearwaters hover and float above a bubble cloud, prepared to feed on fish being driven to the surface by humpback whales.

*Photo courtesy of Dolphin Fleet Whale,
Provincetown, Massachusetts.*

Photo courtesy of Dolphin Fleet Whale,
Provincetown, Massachusetts.

Breaching humpback whale

Breaching humpback whales

Flipper slapping

While feeding around whales, several species of gulls may land on the tip of the whale's head to look for small fish in the water.

The heavily marked head of this humpback whale is nearly covered with barnacles and barnacle scars, on top of and interspersed with the hair follicles or tubercles, making up a less than hydrodynamic surface on the top of the head. Most humpback whales don't have this much "activity" on the top of the head.

A close-up look at the chin of a humpback whale, with its definitive markings, scuffs, barnacles and scars.

The "pelican pouch" appearance of the humpback whale's lower jaw is evident as these whales scoop fish and seawater in a great feeding lunge. The pleats distend and the thin-skinned lower jaw fills with another potential meal. Observe the various scuffing scars.

A humpback in an emphatic lunge as the force of its vertical thrust lifts it missile-like above the sea surface.

Naming Whales

Giving a wild animal a personal name sounds like a silly and unscientific idea. We were always taught that wild animals are wild and that by naming them, they were being called something other than what they were. It turns out, however, it is also a useful way to gather data on individual creatures.

In the mid-1970s, very little was known about the humpback whale, *Megaptera novaeangliae.* These large cetaceans, like so many other species of great whales, had suffered centuries of slaughter and had been declining in world populations. Identification of individual whales was just beginning to be regarded as a way to study populations, seasonal movement, and overall distribution. Techniques like applying tags to large whales and waiting for that individual to be killed by commercial whalers and having that tag returned to the researchers was a slow and fairly unproductive way to gather data on individual whales.

By 1976, a method of identifying individual humpback whales had been developed by an organization called Allied Whale, the marine mammal research facility at the College of the Atlantic in Bar Harbor, Maine. This method involved photographing the underside of a humpback whale's tail. Each time a humpback completes a series of breaths at the surface, it lifts its enormous tail, called a fluke. This fluke may be 10-15 feet wide from tip to tip. As the tail is raised, the underside (ventral fluke) is photographed from behind as it presents a huge, patterned mural to the observer. Like a human fingerprint, the patterns on the ventral fluke are unique to each individual whale and present a convenient way of identification.

The first humpback whale so identified was named Salt, interestingly, not because of a pattern on the underside of the fluke, but because of a pattern of white pigment on the dorsal fin that looked like it was covered with salt. When this whale was seen it was swimming with another large adult that was named, you guessed it, Pepper.

The giant fluke of a humpback whale called Giraffe shows a pattern on the right side that looks like the parallel rows of spots on a giraffe's neck. Giraffe is a large female humpback whale that was first sighted by Provincetown Center for Coastal Studies researchers in 1987. Since that first sighting, she has returned to the northern feeding grounds with five calves.

Several features are visible upon close inspection. I always thought this whale could've been called "Cloud," for the stratus cloud shape on the left side. Note the barnacles on the tip of the right side and the obvious killer whale teeth rake scars on the right side. In 1997, Giraffe gave birth to a calf that, between their departure form the warm birthing waters of the Caribbean and their arrival in the northern feeding grounds, was attacked by killer whales.

Here we see a detail of Giraffe's right fluke, showing the namesake pattern as well as other pigment features. To the right of the orca scars is a smiley face. The cluster of barnacles at the right tip must live a very exciting life, considering their dynamic location.

Giraffe's calf, Okapi, here about 7 months old, was attacked by killer whales during its migration from the Caribbean to the waters off New England. Most noticeable are the scars caused by the orca's teeth over a large part of the flukes. Both sides showed comparable damage. It is one thing to see the scars after numerous tears and puncture wounds have healed, but we can only imagine the traumatic activity, the dynamic energy that was expended by predators and prey in the North Atlantic as this calf struggled to get away. We can only wonder at the time span, depth of the water, the number of orcas, the behavior of Giraffe, and the calf's struggle to survive.

The white dots represent the single tooth punctures of a closed killer whale jaw on the calf's fluke. The calf was named Okapi, after the striped flanks of the African ungulate of that name. Okapi has not been seen since the year of birth, although this is not unusual for humpbacks as they disperse over a huge ocean! *Photo courtesy of Provincetown Center for Coastal Studies.*

This took place off the tip of Cape Cod, near the small fishing village of Provincetown, Massachusetts, where the business of taking people out in commercial party boats to catch fish would soon become the world-wide phenomenon we call whale watching.

Captain Al Avellar noticed that the people on his Dolphin Fleet fishing vessels were spending more time watching the enormous and surface-active humpback whales swimming and feeding near the boat than they were baiting hooks and catching fish. It didn't take long for Captain Avellar to realize that people would come onboard his vessels to see these magnificent creatures, and whale watching was born.

Researchers from the Center for Coastal Studies in Provincetown began accompanying these trips, both as naturalist/educators and researchers, photographing flukes, dorsal fins, scars and other identifiable characteristics of every humpback whale observed. This data, along with the photographs and data from the College of the Atlantic, contributed to what is now the largest humpback whale population study ever carried out. This research continues today with over five thousand individual whales photographed, catalogued and named.

Humpback whales breed and give birth to their young in the warm Caribbean waters off the coast of Puerto Rico and the Dominican Republic. Observers there began to realize that the ventral flukes of humpback whales photographed in these warm waters during the months of December and January, had patterns similar, no, identical, to the patterns of whales summering off the coast of New England. This confirmed that humpback whales migrate from calving and breeding grounds in the Caribbean during the winter months, to feeding grounds in the Gulf of Maine and the western North Atlantic Ocean in warmer summer months.

Humpback whale calves accompany their mothers to these feeding grounds, still nursing on rich, fatty milk, while the mothers gorge themselves on tons of small fish in the cold, oxygen- and nutrient-rich waters of New England and points north. By photographing the ventral flukes of the calves as they swim beside their mothers, who are also photographed, researchers are able to create "family trees" of humpback whales. Male and female humpback whales do not form lasting family relationships and they breed freely with several partners in warm Caribbean waters. The gravid female carries the developing fetus for a gestation period of about a year to the northern feeding grounds in summer and back to the southern waters where the calf is born. The calf stays with its mother for the first year, The father of the calf is unknown, although DNA research on tissue samples may help to solve this parental mystery.

Salt, in the thirty-three years since she was named on the world's first commercial whale watching trip, has returned to the feeding grounds off Cape Cod with eleven calves. She is now a grandmother in the population study, as several of her daughters over the years have had calves of their own. Salt's age is unknown. She was an adult when first sighted and the number of calves she may have had before 1976 is not known.

Other species of great whales, whether rorquals or right whales, are more difficult to individualize, although different types of distinctive patterns are visible and diagnostic.

The Bandit and the flag. Carrying on with a behavior called lob tailing, this mature male humpback whale, called Bandit, was astern of our vessel giving a patriotic backdrop to the ensign flag. Bandit is one of the few humpbacks not named for the pattern on the ventral fluke. Instead, Bandit has two white patches on the dorsal fluke giving the impression of a Zorro-like bandit mask. Bandit is also known for his highly active kick feeding style with lots of swirls and twists after kicking, as he descends into deeper water to corral and capture prey. *Photo courtesy of Provincetown Center for Coastal Studies.*

The distinctive patterns on the ventral surface of whale flukes are used to identify individual whales.

Echo is named for the pattern that looks like sound waves on the lower left fluke. This is actually a scar left from the rows of teeth of a killer whale that at some time harassed and bit this humpback.

The fluke of a humpback Whale called "Dome."

Looking Into the Eye of a Whale

Divers in warm, clear waters of the tropics occasionally may have the privilege of looking into the eye of a great whale, but in the green murky waters of the North Atlantic Ocean, where most of the people who observe a whale are on whale watching vessels, it is a rare occurrence when a humpback whale rolls over at the surface and looks up, out of the water. We do, however, often have this opportunity with the Atlantic white-sided dolphin, the most frequently observed species of *Odontoceti*. Dolphins swim in large social groups called pods, sometimes numbering in the thousands as they move across the fluid plain of the open sea. From a vessel we see them "porpoising," lunging to breathe or to simply break the surface repeatedly as they travel along.

What do they see? Do they comprehend? How do they interpret their vision of us as they pass by, two-legged, active creatures on a large metal hulk, waving their limbs and vocalizing? Even as we look upon the dolphins with adoration and awe, do they think that we are a little strange?

Experiments at large marine mammal training facilities or aquatic parks where dolphins "perform" for audiences have been conducted on a large scale with a variety of stimuli and controlled situations. We have gained most of our knowledge about *Odontocete* sensory perception by studying dolphins and killer whales in these enormous concrete tanks.

I will always gaze in wonder and awe at the eye of a whale. We rarely have the chance. Most eye-to-eye contact we see in photographs or on video is captured under water. I have tried to put myself in situations where I can see the whale looking into *my* world, rather than me swimming below the surface and looking into the eye in the whale's world. It is possible to see the eye of the whale as the whale gazes into the dry world of the human. It makes one wonder what a whale interprets as it sees us? Does it communicate to the other whales about observing these active creatures waving and reaching out?

Here are three images of whale's eyes as three different humpbacks gazed up, out of the water, and I gazed back, first through the lens of my own eye, then through the lens of a camera.

This image of the eye of a juvenile humpback whale was taken a fraction of a second before water swept over the eye. By the time the camera shutter clicked back open, all I saw was water and I thought I had missed the shot. It wasn't until the film was developed weeks later and I took a closer look that I realized I had this beautiful image.

The base of the raised flipper is visible in this image of the eye of a flipper-slapping humpback, another juvenile whale. Note the interesting white patch around part of the eye.

In the great whales, notably the *Mysticetes*, we know less about their underwater perception because we don't have them in captivity and we can't conduct research or experiments to measure their level of visual acuity because controlled situations for research related to sensory perception are virtually nonexistent. What we know about these large whales comes primarily from necropsies of dead whales, where fresh specimens are hard to come by and the tissue is often breaking down or decaying. We have, however, gained enough knowledge from these situations to determine some general anatomical facts about their eyes and visual acuity.

The retinas in the eyes of baleen whales have a higher number of rods than cones. This gives the cetaceans a higher capacity to see in the low light conditions of the deep sea. The cone cells in the retina allow the organism to see color and are less abundant in the whales, limiting their ability to view the full color spectrum and in fact allowing for more green-blue vision than red, which is also absorbed quickly at the sea surface.

It is possible from a vessel to look into the eye of one of the great whales. This is best achieved when a whale is at the surface and rolls on its side, in a behavior called "flipper slapping" (see surface behaviors). When this behavior occurs, the whale's eye is often above the surface and can be seen by the alert observer.

As the whale raises its flipper, there is a bulge or slight hump in the body of the whale, just forward of the point at which the flipper joins the body. This is the protruding mound of the eyeball. Often, people are so taken by the larger vision of the whale's huge mass, that they do not notice the glaring, often foggy and abstract, tennis ball-sized eye looking up at them. It is most often seen in young whales, best in calves, as they readily "play" and roll at the surface.

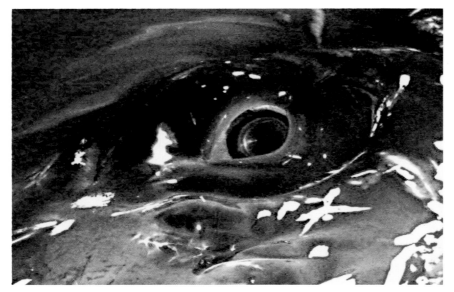

A playful humpback lies on its side showing a wide-open eye during a "close boat approach." This is the rare moment when a whale clearly approaches and appears curious about the boat. Boat engines are shut down and we drift, like an insignificant speck in a million square miles of ocean, while a humpback whale circles it, bumping, rolling, staring, and showing every inch of its body as it lazily twists, turns, and drifts below the boat rails. Captains often say they've been "kidnapped" when a CBA occurs, because they can't move the boat until the whale leaves the area. More than once this has left clock-watching passengers on the dock waiting for a boat that has been held captive by a curious whale.

Photo courtesy of Dolphin Fleet Whale, Provincetown, Massachusetts.

Humpback Whales

One of the most sought after experiences for anyone on a whale watching trip is the sight of humpback whales, *megaptera novaeangliae,* feeding. Nothing is predictable when at sea, so we never know when this high energy, beautifully powerful sequence of events may occur. The huge, pouch-like lower jaw, distended pleats and thousands of gallons of fish-filled sea water, filled with air bubbles, give the surrounding sea an emerald green hue. Close views of the baleen, often worn, sometimes appearing shredded and bent, the pink pallet, or roof of the mouth, barnacles clinging to the jaws and chin, the hair follicles on head and chin, and the truck bed sized lower jaw, filled with thousands of gallons of water are all sights that most humans in the world will never see.

Many of these feeding whales show characteristic scuffs or scars on the front upper jaw from rubbing along the sandy substrate of the sea bottom, forcing sand launce from their hiding places and being consumed by the whales. Look at the range of white scars and red sores. Are the whales "right-handed" or "left-handed?" Each whale characteristically uses either the right or left side of the jaw to scuff with, and tends to show that preference. While there is no consistent time of day for feeding, any observations of this dynamic behavior are treasured by enthusiastic observers.

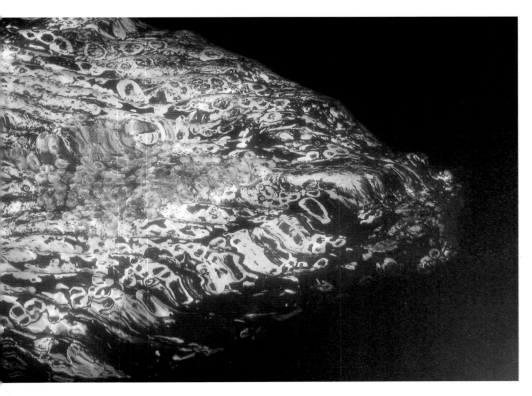

A juvenile humpback whale's chin and throat present a mosaic of barnacles and light refraction during a "close boat approach." This young whale leisurely swam to the side of the boat to the screaming amazement of all on board. It rolled over and stayed belly up, motionless, for half a minute, before slowly swimming under the boat and surfacing on the other side, as people crossed the decks to watch it open its blowholes and drench everyone, mucking up camera lenses and glasses with a blast from its blowholes. This type of seemingly curious behavior by a whale, the "who's watching whom" phenomenon, along with the dynamic surface behaviors for which humpbacks are known, are the amazing once-in-a-lifetime experiences that lure so many thousands to whale watches. *Photo courtesy of Dolphin Fleet Whale, Provincetown, Massachusetts.*

One of the most exciting observations on a whale watch is the sight of a humpback whale mother and calf. The calf, still nursing, gains a tremendous amount of weight drinking very rich, fatty mother's milk. Calves most often stay with their mothers for the first year of life. Like all youngsters, they are playful and curious. Some calves may become independent of mom earlier than expected, before the first summer is over, while others may stay with her longer than usual, even into its second year. *Photo courtesy of Dolphin Fleet Whale, Provincetown, Massachusetts.*

The broad flukes of a humpback whale called Nile, named for the "river" pattern on her fluke. Nile, born to a whale called Mars in 1987, was thought to be a male, after reaching sexual maturity at around five years of age and not being seen with a calf until the age of eleven. At that point, all the data about Nile's gender was changed. Nile's first calf, named Amazon after another great river, made Mars a grandmother. *Photo courtesy of Dolphin Fleet Whale, Provincetown, Massachusetts.*

A humpback whale called "Sockeye" with a deformed lower jaw, the tip of which "curls" upward like the hooked jaw of a sockeye salmon. The baleen in front is deformed due to the shape of the jaw, but still plays the role it was designed for.

61

Right Whales

North Atlantic right whales, *Eubalaena glacialis,* are the rarest of all the great whales, with an estimated population of around 350 individuals left in the world. This less than optimal gene pool, along with the constant threat of ship strikes and entanglement in fishing gear are limiting factors to their survival. In Cape Cod Bay, right whales arrive as early as January, building in numbers through March and sometimes into April and May before continuing north and east into the cold and rich waters of the Bay of Fundy. Cape Cod Bay may support up to a third of the entire population during this 4-month period as they exploit rich clouds of fatty, oily copepods in the cold, oxygen rich waters. Shipping lanes in the United States and Canada have been altered to help assure the survival of this slow moving, seemingly oblivious species. With no dorsal fin, North Atlantic right whales are difficult to see at the surface, adding to the threat of ship strikes throughout their range.

In these two images, right whales court and flirt in Cape Cod Bay on a late winter day.

Minke Whales

The minke whale, like most baleen whales, is a mystery to humans. Its life history, breeding habits, and migration routes are poorly understood. Up until the mid-1970s, many countries sent harpoon boats to sea to kill and harvest whales. International conservation and management of whale populations in the world's oceans has helped in the recovery of whale populations or, at a minimum, prevented the radical decline of several species of baleen whales. Minke whales occur in sustainable numbers and are not endangered in U.S. waters, largely because they were not heavily hunted during the profitable days of whaling. At 25 feet, they are relatively small compared to the other baleen whales. They are quick, agile and very "dolphinesque" in their movement through the water. The scientific name of the minke whale is *Balaenoptera acutarostrata*, which translates as a baleen whale with a pointed nose. They push through the surface almost vertically to exhale then inhale, arching their back sharply and displaying their sleek falcate dorsal fin, then disappear under the water to rise again in 10 seconds or so for another breath. Three to six breaths complete the breathing sequence.

When we observe minke whales on the open sea, the arched back, the well-defined dorsal fin and the quick disappearance are characteristic of this presently hunted baleen whale species.

Finback Whales

The finback, or fin, whale, *Balaenoptera physalus,* is the second largest animal ever to have lived on earth. Its scientific name translates roughly as a baleen whale that spouts like a bellows, referring to its very tall, narrow spout. This gigantic, frequently observed whale is second in size only to the blue whale, which is rare in the waters around Cape Cod. Finback whales are long, tubular, hydrodynamic whales that show only part of the dorsal surface, including the tall, dorsal fin for which they are named, as they glide through the sea. They reach a length of over seventy feet and weigh up to seventy-five tons or more. Finback whales feed on small fish, squid, and a type of euphisid shrimp called krill. Unique in coloration, they display asymmetrical pigmentation, appearing white on the right side of the lower jaw, while having the typical grayish brown of the overall body on the left side. Imagine a tiger with different stripe colors on each side, or a butterfly with different colors on each wing. It has been suggested that this asymmetrical coloration has evolved as a means to corral small fish into a tighter ball through the flashing of bright white as the whale swims clockwise around a school of fish, making it more and more tightly packed. The whale then lunges through the school, mouth open, catching a large amount of biomass as the fish cluster together.

A sleek finback whale in Provincetown Harbor cruises past Long Point Light, at the Cape's tip. *Photo courtesy of Dolphin Fleet Whale, Provincetown, Massachusetts.*

Looking more like a geologic land formation than the jaw line and shadowed eye of a sixty ton whale, this right side view of the face of a fin whale shows the pure white lower jaw and the beginning of the ventral grooves or pleats that extend to the whale's navel. Note the flattened splashguard and closed blowholes on top of the head. This cetacean was gliding slowly about one foot below the surface.

Boat propeller scars on an adult fin whale. The enormous finback whales can lie motionless a foot or two below the surface, making them vulnerable to a fast moving sport or recreational speedboat that can tear right over their backs. On one whale watch boat excursion, we were stopped, out of gear, waiting for one or two finbacks that had been submerged for several minutes. A family of three, parents and a child, slowly cruised into the area aboard a twenty-four foot inboard cruiser. Dad was at the helm and as I called over our vessel's PA system for him to take his boat out of gear, he obliviously got up, and walked to a cooler at the back of his boat, which was still in gear and moving very slowly. There was a shudder below the surface of the water; with concentric rings and little splashes around the boat. The man looked over the side and shrugged. I saw a huge fluke print in the water where the rising whale had kicked hard to dive, and it was over in seconds. We never saw the whale rising, never saw it again. Was there contact? We'll never know. *Photo courtesy of Provincetown Center for Coastal Studies.*

Fin whales, gigantic, hydrodynamic cetaceans, may appear similar to others of the same species at first sighting, but there are distinctions to be made. On some of these "finners" we see diatoms clinging to the body, giving a definitive gold to the streaking side as this, the fastest of the great whales, moves by.

The tall dorsal fin of this whale is tattered and torn, In addition notice the white lower jaw on the right side of the face and the variation of shading.

Blue Whales

The only blue whale, *Balaenoptera musculus,* I've ever seen was too big to photograph. On a routinely awesome day of whale watching off the coast of Cape Cod, a call came over the vessel radio that a blue whale had been spotted. Extremely rare in these waters, this largest of all animals that has ever lived on Earth was on a linear track, moving slow and deliberately, with breathing sequences of 6 to 8 breaths, in a straight line. I have never seen such organized, conservative and I must say, polite behavior between competing whale watching companies from Boston to Cape Cod as each vessel came, people observed as we drifted along side this beautiful, blue dappled and blotched creature, then moved off, one vessel after another. A quick look, a seemingly unconcerned monarch of the ocean, and I, with only a 300mm telephoto lens.

Blue whale

Sei Whales

Another rarely seen species is the sei whale, *Balaenopterus borealis*. Typically, this species remains far off the New England coast in deep open water, but in some years may be found closer to shore. Its name pronounced, "say" refers to a connection with the pollack, a finfish that occurs in Norwegian waters, and is fed upon by this medium sized whale. While hard to identify because of its similarity to a large minke or small fin whale, the sei often swims with a "flat-backed" appearance, not as arched as its close relatives and having sharply defined falcate dorsal fin. They feed on plankton, often rice-sized copepods and small euphausiid shrimp called krill, and are often in the company of the critically endangered northern right whale.

Sei Whale

Dolphins and Porpoises

The majority of the world's whales are not called whales at all. They are called dolphins and porpoises. These are toothed whales, *odontoceti*. The toothed whales have only one blowhole, while the baleen whales clearly show two. The second nostril in toothed whales has evolved into part of the mechanism related to echolocation, so at the area on top of the head we only see one opening or blowhole in the dolphins and porpoises. Dolphins like these Atlantic white-sided dolphins, *Lagenorhynchus acutus,* also give clear observations of their eyes as they lunge to breathe or roll on their sides at the waters surface.

Photo courtesy of Provincetown Center for Coastal Studies.

Photo courtesy of Provincetown Center for Coastal Studies.

Atlantic white-sided dolphins and pilot whales. Neither is considered a "great whale," but this image shows a major difference between them and their larger relatives.

The Scourge of Entanglement

Entanglements occur when marine animals accidentally swim into fishing gear, wrapping the net or line around appendages, fluke and tail stalk (peduncle), or the entire body. These entanglements may come in the form of working gear like gill nets, dragger nets, and lobster lines or any kind of line or monofilament. In today's world, a high percentage of this gear is made of polypropylene line. This whale-killing cable doesn't stretch, doesn't break, and doesn't decompose. A whale that runs into a submerged line with a flipper, a thrust of the tail, or, worse, an open mouth while feeding is likely to react initially with panic, becoming even more entangled, and then may swim dragging any amount of netting or gear for long periods of time, days, weeks or months. Some whales are lucky enough to be saved because they are observed and reported to an organization like the Provincetown Center for Coastal Studies out of Provincetown, Massachusetts, or any member organizations of the Atlantic Large Whale Disentanglement Network in the United States or Canada. Their impressive efforts have saved many entangled whales, but in a million square miles of north Atlantic Ocean, many whales are likely to die after long slow exhaustive efforts to free themselves.

On any whale watching outing, humpback whales can be observed with scars, V-notches, and even open wounds from entanglement in lines or nets. Working gillnet sets are anchored to the bottom and often have floating or buoyant anchor lines attached to the net. A one-hundred foot long gillnet set, about 10 feet high, will not stop the momentum of a 50 ton whale that accidently swims into it in the dark sea. The net, a part of it or the entire rig may be torn from the bottom, wrapping the animal. Other monofilament gillnets may be torn from their anchors and float freely in the open sea. These are called ghost nets.

State and federal laws to protect marine life are on the books, and fishermen have made concentrated efforts to alter and make changes to coastal and deep-water gear in an effort to cut down on the entanglement. "Pingers" are small acoustic devises that warn dolphins and porpoises of the presence of nets, and have cut down on the "by catch" of these animals in recent years. But the marine environment is too expansive and monitoring is extremely difficult despite the best efforts of all involved. Animals continue to become entangled. Diving birds, seals, and other marine organisms become entangled in this gear despite efforts to prevent the entanglements due to modification of gear. Millions of birds become entangled in nets and line each year when they dive beneath the surface to feed. Seals are protected in the United States under the Marine Mammal Protection Act, thereby causing a sharp increase in their populations. Both gray seals and harbor seals become entangled in nets and other fishing gear. The practice of "hauling out" on sandy or rocky shores allows observers to locate entangled seals and these marine mammals may be disentangled by rescue organizations.

People always ask, "What happens when whales die?" Of course there are many answers to this question. Most probably just sink and are eaten by a great diversity of sea life eventually breaking down to organic bottom sediment. Some wash up on beaches where, depending on the level of decomposition, scientists may glean information about the anatomy and physiology of an animal rarely encountered for close, terrestrial investigation. In this case a 20-24 foot minke whale was found floating off the coast of Massachusetts. A group of blue sharks were tearing the carcass apart. Here the whale is floating belly up and the lower jaw has been eaten back to the chest blubber. The yellow plates of baleen can be seen extending from the remaining upper jaw. The smell of the carcass was making people on our whale watching boat sick and many were upset that we would stop to observe such a gruesome sight, but the power and grace of the sharks was truly impressive. *Photo courtesy of Provincetown Center for Coastal Studies.*

This humpback appears to be dragging fishing gear, but, upon closer examination, the "gear" is nothing more than organic material that was picked up by the whale as it swam through a dense mass of algae, eel grass, or other marine plant material. The material is wrapped around the left fluke but not around the peduncle or tail stalk, which would be an indicator of a potentially life-threatening entanglement. Closer examination determined that there is no man-made material, so it's likely the material simply slid off the fluke. *Photo courtesy of Provincetown Center for Coastal Studies.*

Here is an example of the situation that occurs when seals become entangled in fishing gear. This type of neck and head entanglement may occur under a number of circumstances. A seal may swim accidentally into a net, it may become entangled while "stealing" fish from active fishing gear, or the monofilament gill net may have torn loose from a bottom set or was discarded, floating freely and accidentally entangling the seal. These types of entanglement may be fatal due to constriction of the airways and esophagus or from infection as the non-biodegradable monofilament cuts into the fur and flesh.

Whales and other marine mammals are not exclusive to net entanglements. This male red-breasted merganser washed ashore in a cluster of fishing net. These diving ducks that feed almost exclusively on fish, migrate to coastal waters in the non-breeding season and appear by the thousands along the coastline of New England. This male was collected on a Cape Cod beach in winter. From its appearance in a small piece of netting, it may have been cut loose from a larger net. Millions of diving birds become entangled each year as they chase small fish, and may completely foul extensive amounts of netting and gear, rendering it ineffective and useless for catching fish.

A deep notch and scar on the tail stalk, or peduncle, of this humpback whale indicates that it spent time wrapped in line, perhaps dragging gear behind or below it. The line, often made of non-biodegradable polypropylene digs into the whale's flesh and leaves a permanent notch. The white pigment on the leading edge of the flukes represents the healed abrasion caused by the constant rubbing of the line. *Photo courtesy of Provincetown Center for Coastal Studies.*

The notch and swollen scar on the tail stalk after this whale was entangled in rope or other line for a long period, causing the line to dig into the flesh and leave a notched scar.

Further Reading

Clapham, P. *Humpback Whales.* Voyageur Press, 1996.

Coffey, D. J. *Dolphins, Whales and Porpoises. An Encyclopedia of Sea Mammals.* Macmillan Publishing Co., Inc., 1977.

Ellis, Richard. *The Book of Whales.* Alfred A. Knopf, Inc., 1980.

Harrison, L. Matthew. *The Natural History of the Whale.* Columbia University Press, 1978.

Robbins, Jooke and David K. Mattila. "Monitoring entanglements of humpback whales (Megaptera novaeangliae) in the Gulf of Maine on the basis of caudal peduncle scarring." Unpublished report to the 53rd Scientific Committee Meeting of the International Whaling Commission. Document#SC/53/NAH25. Available from the Provincetown Center for Coastal Studies, Provincetown, MA 02657 USA, 2001.

Katona, Steven K., Valerie Rough, and David T. Richardson. *A Field Guide to Whales, Porpoises, and Seals from Cape Cod to Newfoundland.* Smithsonian Institution Press, 1993.

Leatherwood, Steven, and Randall R. Reeves. *Whales and Dolphins.* Sierra Club Books, 1983.

McNulty, Faith. *The Great Whales.* New York: Harper & Row, 1980.

Slijper, Everhard J. *Whales and Dolphins.* University of Michigan Press, 1976.

Watson, Lyall. *Sea Guide to Whales of the World.* E.P. Dutton, 1981.

This is the dorsal fin of a whale named Salt, the grand dame of all humpback whales. She was the first humpback whale ever named in the world. The first whale watching trip was aboard a Dolphin Fleet vessel in 1976. This was the first whale that was observed on that voyage. The white pigmentation over the dorsal fin looks like a patch of salt. She has been seen every year since 1976 and has returned to the waters around Cape Cod with eleven different calves over those years. Two of her daughters have had calves of their own, making Salt a grandmother.

Organizations

- American Cetacean Society: www.acsonline.org/
- Cetacean Alliance: www.cetaceanalliance.org
- International Fund for Animal Welfare (IFAW): www.IFAW.org
- Marine Connection: www.marineconnection.org
- New England Coastal Wildlife Alliance: www.necwa.org
- New England Aquarium: www.neaq.org
- Provincetown Center for Coastal Studies: www.coastalstudies.org
- Whale Center of New England: whalecenter.org
- Whale and Dolphin Conservation Society (WDCS: wdcs.org